The Project Manager's

SURVIVAL GUIDE

the handbook
for real-world project management

Donald D. Penner

Second Edition

BATTELLE PRESS
Columbus • Richland

02-1531

Library of Congress Cataloging-in-Publication Data

Penner, Donald D., 1938-
   The project manager's survival guide: the handbook for real-world project management
/ Donald Penner. – 2nd ed.
      p. cm.
   Includes bibliographical references and index.
   ISBN 1-57477-126-4 (alk. paper)
      1. Project management. I. Title: Survival guide. II. Title.

HD69.P75P46 2002
658.4'04–dc21   2001056623

Editing and book design:
      First Edition – Karen Anderson, UnCommon Sense, Seattle
      Second Edition – Kristin Manke and Amy Madden, Battelle Press, Columbus

Printed in the United Sates of America

Battelle Press
505 King Avenue
Columbus, Ohio 43201-2693
614-424-6393; 1-800-451-3543
Fax: 614-424-3819
Web Bookstore: www.battelle.org/bookstore
E-mail: press@battelle.org

Foreword

The Project Manager's Survival Guide is more than a book. It's a management tool for your desk and your briefcase.

It's there to help you with the most critical decisions you'll make as a manager: What to take on. How to launch a project. How to spot problems—and address them—long before the crisis stage. How to handle a crisis when it does occur.

The *Survival Guide* reflects Don Penner's experience as a manager, researcher, consultant, and teacher. Don first sketched the *Survival Guide* in outline form for a training program Battelle designed and conducted for project and program managers.

Referring to it as a "never-finished draft," Don updates the *Survival Guide* continuously to reflect problems that arise and strategies that work in real-world organizations. The handbook's reminders, checklists, self-evaluations, and refreshingly frank comments ("Tell the truth—*always"*) do more than prepare a project manager for tough terrain. They guide you, step by step, through the thick of it.

The *Survival Guide* has been so popular among Battelle clients that we urged Don to let us make it available to a general business audience. We are proud to present this easy-to-use desktop edition.

Joseph Sheldrick, Publisher

Preface

From the beginning, *The Project Manager's Survival Guide* was intended as a list of ideas and thoughts—reminders about the things that are easy to forget but which always seem to come back and "bite" even the most experienced project manager.

Many of these reminders come from executives, line managers, and project managers we have interviewed about their real-world experiences in project management. At the conclusion of each interview, we asked them to list the primary ways that projects, and project managers, get in trouble. Several chapters of the *Survival Guide* conclude with excerpts from these interviews.

Nearly everyone we interviewed emphasized that when problems arise in a project, the project manager should report these difficulties to his or her manager *as soon as they are discovered.* Several executives pointed out that when they find out about problems after the fact, their reactions are likely to be frustration and anger. Had they been informed early on, they would have been in a position to help deal with the problem.

The *Survival Guide* was originally designed to accompany a weeklong seminar designed by Battelle for project and program managers. Thanks are due to Steve Ford and Pat Bettin with whom I collaborated on the development of the seminar. We spent many productive hours discussing project management.

I would also like to thank the executives, managers, and project team members of the many client organizations that I have worked with, as well as the more than 500 individuals who participated in our weeklong project management courses in the US and abroad. I learned at least as much from them as they learned from our seminars.

Since the first edition of the *Survival Guide* was published in 1994, I have spent most of my time involved in a series of international projects. Thus, this second edition includes a chapter dealing with some of the unique aspects of such projects. I have also replaced the Assessment of Team-Oriented Leadership with a new, shorter, and more carefully focused assessment instrument. In addition, I have attempted to clarify a number of points throughout the *Survival Guide* that some people found a bit confusing.

Kristin Manke did an excellent job editing this second edition, and as usual, Joe Sheldrick, the publisher, provided the pushing and prodding to bring this second edition to fruition. I thank them both.

Finally, I thank Carolyn, my wife, for her encouragement and for putting up with the many nights and weekends I have devoted to this and other projects since we were married in 1961.

Donald D. Penner

Contents

The Project Manager's

SURVIVAL
GUIDE

Before you take the job

1. Getting Started

Before you take on an assignment as a project manager, especially if it is your first opportunity as a manager, it is important to ask yourself a few questions and collect information about the project. Executives tell us that one of the main reasons projects fail is a poor match between the project and the project manager. They also tell us that, too often, potential project managers get sold on attempting to manage impossible projects.

Remember that it is one thing to agree to attempt to run a three-minute mile but another thing to do it. Even though turning down the opportunity to manage a high-visibility project is a career risk, it is almost always less risk than taking on a project that is doomed to failure. So, before you take on a project:

Assess your personal situation

Assess your own motivation and ability to be a project manager. Is this something you want to do? Does it make sense to you?

1

Project management is very different from doing technical work as an individual contributor. Listed below are just a few ways in which project management differs from technical work:

Which type of position is best for you?

Project Manager	Individual Contributor
Large span of control	Relatively small span of control
Many subordinates	Few subordinates
High people and budget component	High technical or engineering component
Surrounded by technical experts	Requires "hands on" expertise
As many as 200 activities/day	Limited number of activities/day
Many interruptions	Few interruptions
Time for interactions	Time for reading and analyzing
Serves as "boss" to team	Serves as facilitator to team
Career = management advancement	Career = growth in field
Much intervention in lives of others	Little exercise of power required
High stress	Lower stress

A project management job is often a first step into a management career. However, in many organizations, project managers are not considered to be part of "management." In fact, projects often cause difficulty for "management." Because projects, by definition, are not part of the normal flow of business activity, they often get in the way of this normal flow. Projects are most often staffed with personnel "drafted" or recruited from the teams supervised by "management." They also tend to draw other resources away from "management." Project managers usually report to one or more members of "management." Thus, there is often some tension between project managers and line management. Thus, throughout this book, the term "management" is used to refer to the line management of the organization.

Discuss your prospective role with your family.

Project management demands near total commitment of your time. It may also demand relocation and/or extensive travel. This is, of course, especially true if you are being asked to manage an international project.

Ask yourself "Do I have a choice?"

In a real sense, you always have a choice. Slavery was outlawed years ago. On the other hand, you may be in a situation where, if you want to keep your job, you must take on the project.

If the project management job description has elements you dislike but can live with, then go ahead. You may find that once you get into the job you will actually come to enjoy it. For many people, project management is an exciting, satisfying job.

After you have assessed your personal situation, the next steps are as follows:

Assess the project situation

Gather information about the project.

At this stage it is important to determine if the project is reasonable or if you are being asked to run a three-minute mile. Consider the following elements:

1. Technical requirements

Have similar things been done in the past? Will you be pressing the "state of the art"? Will the project require development of new technology? Are the technical requirements reasonably clear or is there a lot of ambiguity? The requirements for some projects are akin to "Bring me a rock, and when you do I'll tell you if it is the right rock."

2. Schedule

Is the proposed schedule attainable? Will it be a race from beginning to end or is there some leeway? Remember Mr. Murphy and his laws?

Norman Augustine, former president of Martin Marietta Corporation, has compiled a number of similar laws in his book *Augustine's Laws.* Law XXII states, "Any task can be completed in only one-third more time than is currently estimated." He bases this assertion on his analysis of more than 100 projects conducted for the US government's aerospace program.

3. Budget

Do the current budget estimates appear reasonable? Do you have a management reserve to deal with unknown contingencies?

4. Resources

What about other resources, such as the availability of space, equipment, computers, staff support, etc.?

5. Risk

What is the level of risk in the project? There are many forms of risk. Some of these are discussed later in the chapter on planning (Chapter 6).

How about career risk? What is the payoff to you if the project is a success? What are the costs if it goes down the tubes?

6. Management

Does the project have the right kind and amount of line management attention and commitment?

7. Customers/Users

Does the project have "good" customers/users? Do they want the project or must they be "sold" on it? Do they know what they want? "Bring me a rock" is often encountered with customers/users.

8. The project team

Can you, and will you be allowed to, assemble a capable, motivated project team? Too often team members are assigned because of their availability rather than because of their skill and ability.

If your answers to these eight questions lead you to decide that the project is unrealistic and has little chance of success, *speak up now.* There will never be a better time to discuss the problems and let management know that this project is doomed.

Negotiate your charter

If you do projects for outside clients, the contract with the client is the charter for the project. It spells out the terms and conditions under which you will do the work.

For an internal project, the charter is the understanding you must reach with senior or line management. It spells out the terms and conditions under which you will do the project.

In all but the smallest of projects, the charter should be more than just a verbal understanding. You don't need a formal document, but you will need something in writing that defines elements such as:

1. Accountability

Who is answerable for satisfactory completion of the project and for completion of specific assignments within or related to the project? What are the standards against which the success of the project will be judged?

2. Authority

What formal power has been granted to you and others (possibly by their position) to make final decisions relative to the project? From whom do you derive your formal authority?

How broad is your authority? Can you hire and fire project team members? Can you approve travel requests? Can you hire consultants? Can you re-allocate budget?

3. Responsibility

What obligations or promises have individuals incurred relative to the project?

4. **Resources**

   What are the overall budget and schedule within which
   the project must be conducted? What people, facilities,
   equipment, etc., will be available to you?

5. **Support**

   Have other parts of the organization or other individuals
   been tasked to provide input to the project? Who will
   handle administrative, clerical, and secretarial duties?
   Who will pay for such support? Is this support covered
   by overhead or must it be part of the project budget? In
   some projects, the client organization expects to provide
   the bulk of the human resources. If this is the case with
   your project, it is especially important to ensure that the
   contract/charter spells out, in detail, the arrangements for
   this support.

6. **Access and visibility**

   To what degree can you, and are you, expected to
   consult with senior management during the course of the
   project? Where does the project stand on your
   organization's priority list? To whom do you report, and
   how often?

   Who are the power brokers relative to the project? Do
   they support the project? Will you have access to them?

7. **Constraints**

   What are the boundaries within which you must work?
   Consider technical, budget, schedule, and political
   constraints. Also examine *operational* constraints.
   These include situations in which you must use existing
   equipment, interface with a different software system, or

have access to production staff but avoid interfering with on-going operations.

It is extremely important to clarify your charter with your senior management as well as with your customer or client. The whole point of the charter is to reduce ambiguity and to avoid misunderstandings later in the project cycle.

How to get in trouble

1. Not knowing the right things to do

2. Lacking experience

3. Underestimating technical difficulty

4. Making overly optimistic assumptions and ground rules during conceptualization and planning—*agreeing to run the three-minute mile*

5. Not getting or developing clear statements of requirements

6. Getting too involved in technical rather than managerial aspects of the project

7. Failing to obtain a clear charter

"President of the Project"

2. The Project Manager's Role

The project manager has responsibility for the what, when, why, and funding of project requirements as well as for the who, how, and where of project execution.

This chapter spells out the project manager's responsibilities and examines the related issues of formal and personal authority. A leadership skills questionnaire will help you assess your readiness for the project manager's role.

Responsibilities

- Establishing a uniform interpretation of the project requirements—also known as vision

- Developing a comprehensive plan to meet the requirements

- Staffing the project with qualified people in needed disciplines

- Obtaining adequate funding to accomplish the project

- Allocating the work requirements into discrete work elements with definable interfaces

- Defining and assigning interface responsibilities between the work elements

- Assigning the work elements to projects, functional project groups, subcontractors, and vendors

- Providing adequate resources to accomplish each work element on schedule

- Maintaining a continuous overview of project progress so that timely corrective action can be taken when necessary

- Accomplishing both the technical and business objectives of the project

- Keeping management and users up to date on project progress and status against the schedule

- Maintaining control of schedule, cost, and performance (project quality)

- Knowing, understanding, and working cooperatively with the customer complex—management and users/owners—both as organizations and individuals

- Working with management and users/owners to keep the project sold within the customer complex

- Serving as the focal point for technical and business liaisons with all constituencies

- Realizing the full potential of the project.

Authority

Most organizations expect the project manager to fully assume the authority and responsibilities delegated to him or her. The project manager is expected to use this authority as a tool for project success.

"A project manager must have authority. Without it, he/she will not be effective. A potentially good project manager will try to achieve results, but without authority, all he will do is upset himself, other managers, and the organization in general. In addition to assigning him decision-making authority, top management must assign the project manager control over the resources to do the job."

— Charles Martin

Defining the authority of your position

- What are the constraints?
- From whom do you derive your formal authority?
- How broad is your authority in reality?
- What about the power brokers?

    Who are they?

    How do you gain access?

    How far will they support you?

Personal authority

I have never talked to a project manager who felt that he or she had enough authority. Usually, they are thinking only in terms of the *formal authority* that comes with the position of project manager. Because projects, by their very nature, are not part of the line management system, the formal authority granted to project managers is usually less than that granted to comparable line managers. Therefore, project managers must often rely on their *personal authority,* which is a reflection of:

Experience

Knowledge

Reputation

Ability to persuade

Ability to resolve conflicts

Ability to get things done

In other words, personal authority derives from your leadership ability as perceived by relevant people in your organization.

Evaluating your leadership skills

Battelle has developed a model of effective, team-oriented leadership, based on our work with managers in organizations in the US and abroad. The model includes these dimensions:

Personal attributes and characteristics such as integrity, competence, and drive.

Focus on and knowledge of your own organization and the client or customer organization.

People leadership both to achieve teamwork and to meet the developmental and other needs of individual team members.

Task leadership including your decision-making skills and the ability to achieve team productivity.

To evaluate individual leadership preparedness, Battelle has developed a questionnaire for collecting and summarizing perceptions concerning these dimensions. In a formal evaluation, perceptions are collected from people with a variety of perspectives on an individual's skills. Forms are completed by the manager's boss or bosses, peers, team members or subordinates, and customers—as well as by the individual being assessed. Battelle staff analyze the data and prepare a lengthy report summarizing the results.

Appendix A includes a sample questionnaire that you can use to assess your own effectiveness. It should help you in defining your areas of strength and those areas in which you may need further development.

How to get in trouble

1. Failing to understand the responsibilities and role of the project manager

2. Failing to take decisive action when needed

3. Not taking an active leadership role

4. Expecting others to make tough decisions

5. Not keeping management, customers, and team members informed

3. Vision

The *vision* of the project is your conceptual design of the project's end product. It is like the initial sketches provided by an architect after the first set of discussions with the client. In developing this concept, you should answer questions such as:

- What is the project supposed to achieve?

- What are the needs of the client organization?

- What is attainable within the budget and schedule?

- What will your organization and the client organization be like *after* the project is completed?

The military estimate of the situation

The US Army uses a procedure called the "estimate of the situation" to develop an overall conceptualization of the tactical environment. It can be used in a project with the appropriate translation of terms. The military estimate of the situation takes into consideration:

1. Friendly forces, their capabilities and their disposition

2. Enemy forces, their capabilities and their disposition

3. The alternative courses of action

4. The advantages of each course of action

5. The costs or disadvantages of each course of action

Key elements

Certain elements are essential to developing the project vision. Be sure to take into account:

The users

They are your customers. *Treat them that way.* Involve them when you are developing the project concept.

The project mission

How will achievement of the project mission contribute to organizational objectives and strategic initiatives?

How will it contribute to divisional and functional goals?

Product implementation

Is implementation of the project's product in the users' business plans? *If not, why not?*

How to get in trouble

1. Failure to understand the nature of the project

2. Unwillingness to recognize constraints on the project

3. Inability to simplify

4. Lack of accurate assessment of project resources

5. Incomplete understanding of the scope or goals of the project

6. Failure to estimate certain elements

7. Ignorance of the critical issues that can kill the project

8. Inadequate staffing

4. Defining Goals and Objectives

Early on in the project, you will define goals, objectives, and resources as you prepare and refine proposal documents for the customer/user. This chapter lists key elements that should be considered at each stage of the definition process.

Initial proposal

- Determine needs
- Develop concepts
- Define problem
    1. Identify problem
    2. Investigate/verify problem
    3. Write detailed problem statement
- Develop and assess alternative approaches to solving the problem
- Review technical feasibility
- Do a cost/benefit analysis
- Develop an initial proposal

Final proposal

- Hold a preliminary review for all concerned parties
- Conduct a product design analysis for each project product
- Conduct a system analysis to provide the context for the products
- Develop the final proposal

Final statement of work

- Define integration requirements
- Develop a preliminary requirements document
- Define deliverables – *examples*:

    Hardware

    Software

    Specifications drawings

    Drawings

    Test requirements

    Test reports

    Schematics

    Wiring diagrams

    Functional tests

    Training plan

- Complete an engineering work statement
- Finalize the requirements document
- Develop the final statement of work

Approval

- Obtain customer and other necessary approvals

Assessing functional resources

An assessment of the available resources is critical to project efficiency and success. You will want to thoroughly examine:

Divisional management resources

Business management resources

Technical resources

Engineering support resources

Procurement resources

How to get in trouble

1. Not getting or developing clear statements of requirements

5. Ownership

Ownership of the project is arguably the most important factor in project success or failure. This is because owners behave differently than non-owners. Think about the way a homeowner, as opposed to a tenant, deals with maintenance problems. The same concept applies to projects. If senior management, the project manager, the project team, sub-contractors, and the customers feel that they all own the project, they will be committed to its success.

The project manager must ensure that key partners—management, users, and the project team—invest in the project and experience ownership. To do this, the project manager must sell the project.

Selling the project and keeping it sold

Plan for selling the project.

Plan for keeping it sold. Budget time and energy.

Figure out how to work with senior managers who may have different agendas.

Consider the potential owners for your project. Ask:

Do they need the product of your project?

Do they currently want your product?

Will they "pull" the product out of you, or must you "push" it on them?

Develop an owner interface/communication plan.

Include management, staff, subcontractors, and customers.

Ownership and the product users

Find out how the users are organized.

Who are the decision makers?

What are their backgrounds?

Who on your team knows them?

Understand their business.

Understand how they do business now and how they plan to do business in the future.

Understand their needs.

What are their needs with respect to your project, and beyond your project?

Consider employing "one-level-up" system engineering to help understand the technical problem. *Consider the system in which the problem your project addresses exists. Will changes "one-level-up" enhance the product?*

Consider the political realities for your customers.

What drives their decisions?

For what are they rewarded?

For what are they punished?

If you were in their position, would you support your project?

To understand the effects of your project on the users, conduct a cost/benefit analysis from their point of view.

Short-term

Long-term

Positive

Negative

Find out how you can help the users support your project.

Develop rapport and keep your users happy.

- Avoid surprises—be reliable, professional, and businesslike.

- Make them look good—*always*.

- Observe their organizational chain of command—do not bypass people.

- Deliver information and products on time.

- Be ready to educate the users when required.

- Always tell the truth.

- Accept their "nitpicks" and get on with the job.

- Establish your credibility early—or it will be too late.

- Keep them updated. Never surprise them with information—good or bad—that you have had for weeks.

- Anticipate their needs before they occur.

- Fully support their high-level briefings and reviews.

  These can make or break a project.

- Encourage your team members to develop and maintain close working relationships with their user counterparts.

- Treat lower-level user representatives the same way that you treat those at the highest level.

- Share information in advance of meetings.

  This makes the users look good to their bosses.

  It helps keep the meetings orderly.

- Visit the users' facilities and "walk the floor."

  This gives you a feel for their operation and encourages one-on-one discussions.

- Get the users to work your problems.

  Use the rapport you have established.

  Involve them early.

  Work together.

  Remember: Your problem is their problem, and your success is their success.

Ownership and your project team

Remember that the project team members should also be owners.

Begin with a sign-on ceremony.

Establish the level of participation in decisions—who, when, and how much?

Make it clear that people who do the work do the briefings and get the credit.

Consider the issue of individual versus group recognition.

Remember to celebrate successes.

How to get in trouble

1. Failing to clarify the issue of ownership with the customers

2. Underestimating people issues involved in cultural change

3. Omitting to involve all parties as owners

4. Proceeding without buy-in from users

5. Proceeding without commitment from executive management

6. Focusing on the customer at the management level and forgetting about the end-user of a product or service— people who must use the system but who may be resistant to change and concerned with job security

7. Forgetting to keep top brass involved with the project

8. Failing to keep the customer informed and committed

6. Planning

This chapter is about complexity, and all the things you can't afford to forget.

Projects are complex undertakings. If the project is to be completed on schedule and on budget, and is to meet the quality requirements, a detailed project plan is required. The plan must consider all of the complexity. Problems deriving from inaccurate estimates of time, money, and technical difficulty are very minor compared to the problems deriving from factors that no one remembered to include in the plan.

There are two major types of planning—*forward planning* and *backward planning.* Backward planning is the most common type of project planning. In backward planning, you begin with a clear definition or description of the final product and then work backward figuring out what steps are necessary to create that final product. Building a house is a good example of this type of project. You begin with a set of drawings that specify all of the requirements for the finished house. Then you figure out what tasks, resources, etc., will be necessary to build the house. This type of project plan is reasonably easy to develop and, in fact, this type of project is relatively easy to manage as there is little ambiguity.

Forward planning is used when the end product of the project is not well defined. A research project aimed at developing a new cancer drug might be a typical example. There is still a clear vision—a new, effective drug. However, there is no set of drawings and specifications for this new drug. Thus, it is necessary to start the planning process at the beginning by laying out a series of steps designed to move in the correct direction. Such a project plan will probably have a series of decision points where progress will be reviewed and decisions made about how best to proceed. This type of project is characterized by great ambiguity. The project plan may only be a broad outline of the process to be followed with broad estimates of time, budget, and resource requirements. In such a project it is extremely critical to identify the risks involved and to make sure that everyone involved is aware of the these risks.

For both types of projects, a critical part of project planning is the development of a work breakdown structure that depicts the work or activities required to complete the project as best it can be described. In the case of building a house, the various tasks can be described in considerable detail—prepare the site, dig the basement, build the foundation, etc. In the case of developing a new drug, the tasks will be less well defined and described in more general terms—review existing literature, select a potential class of compounds, *in vitro* testing, etc.

Develop work breakdown structure (WBS)

The WBS is a product-oriented family tree or outline that depicts the work required to complete the project. If you are not familiar with the idea of a WBS, consult one or more available textbooks on project management. Most such texts include an extensive discussion. Most project management software programs are set up to facilitate the development of a WBS. For the current purposes only a brief outline of the process is presented here.

1. Start with the most general categories of the project work and continue to break down each category into more and more detail.

2. Each part of the project should be subdivided into the number of levels useful for managing the project.

3. The bottom level should be made up of work packages that can be assigned to a single organization or individual.

4. Each bottom-level work package should include a clear product or deliverable.

5. No effort should be made to extend the WBS to the same number of levels for all project tasks. Some tasks are far more complex than others.

6. Timing relationships, dependencies, and sequences should *not* be considered in developing the WBS.

Responsibility matrix

Using the bottom-level WBS work packages, develop a matrix that shows who will be responsible for completing each work package.

1. Your organization – Within your own organization the responsibility matrix should show the individuals who will be involved in completing each work package.

2. Interfacing organizations – For other organizations or subcontractors you may not be able to develop as detailed a responsibility matrix. However, it is critical that you identify the individuals in these organizations who will be accountable for completion of the assigned or contracted packages of work.

Prepare estimates

Armed with the list of work packages from the WBS and the responsibility matrix, the next step is to prepare estimates. By involving the individuals and organizations actually doing the work in the estimation process, you will increase the accuracy of your estimates.

1. Labor (headcount) – the number of people involved in doing each work package and the amount of time each individual will spend.

2. Dollar costs – the cost of labor, materials, and other resources for each work package.

3. Time (duration) – the elapsed time required for the completion of each work package.

When you receive estimates from project team members or from subcontractors it is important to be careful in attempting to negotiate lower estimates. While it is reasonable to anticipate that there may be some padding in the estimates, by and large the estimates are best guesses of what will be required. It is often fairly easy to get someone to give you a lower estimate. However, there is no guarantee that the new estimate is attainable. Don't forget the parable of the "three-minute mile."

Prepare network diagrams

The network diagrams are made up of the bottom-level work packages from the WBS arranged to show durations, sequences, and dependencies. The network diagrams should indicate when each work package can be started, how long it will take, and when it will be finished. In addition, they should depict relationships between work packages—for example, in building construction you cannot begin putting up the walls until you have poured the foundation and given the concrete time to set.

It is often helpful to write a short description of each package of work on a 3 x 5 card or on a self-adhesive note. Then use these cards to work out the appropriate sequence of work by placing them on a wall. Move the cards around until you are satisfied that you have the best arrangement of the work to be done. This method lets you view the entire project as a whole.

Prepare GANTT charts

GANTT charts are bar charts showing the schedule of work packages on a timeline or calendar.

Tactical planning

1. Detail planning
2. How you will operate from day to day

Risk assessment, analysis, and management

Risk assessment is the process of estimating the risk associated with a particular alternative course of action.

Risk analysis is the generation of alternative courses of action for reducing risk.

Risk management is the process of combining risk analysis with risk assessment in an iterative cycle to generate a minimum-risk course of action.

This section will help you with the critical task of breaking out the risk of doing the project work. Make sure that everyone involved with the project understands the risks involved.

It is particularly important to identify early in the planning process any known or anticipated sources of risk. Remember that, in addition to those risks that you can identify and anticipate, there are almost always risks that you and your team will overlook. These are the dreaded "UNK-UNKs"—the unknown unknowns.

Risk conditions

Technical risk conditions

Materials and device risks

Design risks

Production risks

Programmatic risk conditions

Schedule risks

Planning risks

Project implementation risk conditions

Human resource risks

Management risks

User/customer risk conditions

Needs/requirements change

Business processes change

Political changes

The project plan outline

This section suggests an outline for a typical major project plan. It is not intended to be a template but rather an example of the complexity of a large-scale project.

Introduction

Vision

Background

Project overview

Scope, goals, and objectives

Project work statement

Impact to business process

Goals

Objectives

Project interdependencies

Assumptions, limitations, and constraints

Deliverables

Each of the intermediate products and reports that will be delivered to the customer and/or to senior management

Project strategies and tactics

Development

Implementation and conversion

Cultural and organizational

Risks and abatement plans

Technical risks

Programmatic risks

Implementation risks

User/customer risks

Management plan

Organizational structure, roles, and responsibilities

Steering council/boards/committees

Project manager

Deputy project manager

Process owner(s)

Subproject or task manager(s)

Project sustaining manager(s)

Work breakdown structure

Master phasing plan

Project change control

Project directives

Tracking and visibility

Control mechanism

Status review process

Project resource requirements

Labor and skills

Hardware and software

Facilities

Vendor support/development

Tools

Sustaining plan

Organizational responsibilities

Sustaining/maintenance procedures

Resource requirements

Standards

Documentation plan

Cost/benefit analysis

How to get in trouble

1. Failing to have and use a good business plan

2. Not developing the project plan outline (this is the project manager's responsibility)—the team can't do it, but it must involve them

3. Not making a detailed plan, including schedules, budgets, and resource requirements

4. Not planning for implementation, training, education, etc., upfront

5. Failing to have frequent reviews of the plan by stakeholders. You need to get it in front of people, and the earlier the better

6. Deviating from the plan rather than changing the plan. Losing project configuration control

7. Forgetting to estimate key elements

8. Not seeing or understanding risk

9. Compressing schedules

10. Failing to control change

11. Mitigating requirements

12. Receiving weak performance from technical support groups

13. Receiving technical support groups with weak capabilities

14. Making illogical decisions

15. Receiving inadequate performance from subcontractors or vendors

7. *Organizing and Staffing*

Project management is designed to make better use of existing resources by getting work to flow horizontally as well as vertically within the company. This approach does not destroy the vertical, bureaucratic flow of work, but simply requires that line organizations talk to one another horizontally, so work will be accomplished more smoothly throughout the organization. The vertical flow of work is still the responsibility of the line managers. The horizontal flow of work is the responsibility of the program and project managers, and their primary effort is to communicate and coordinate activities horizontally between the line organizations.

Organizing

The fundamental logic of organizing

Establishment of project objectives

Formulation of derivative objectives

Identification and classification of activities necessary to accomplish the objectives

Grouping these activities in the light of human and material resources available and the best way of using them

Delegating to the head of each group the authority necessary to perform the activities

Tying these groupings together horizontally and vertically, through authority relationships and information systems

Activities for organizing project responsibilities

Clarify responsibilities, authority, and accountability.

Provide job descriptions and detail each staff member's primary purpose.

Who makes what kinds of decisions?

Construct project responsibility flowchart.

Define spans of control.

Don't be responsible for too many people.

Don't be responsible for too few people.

Delegate the authority needed to carry out responsibilities.

Organization design and structure

Differentiation and integration

Differentiation is the degree to which specialization in project elements occurs. That is, how many projects, subprojects, and tasks are required?

Integration provides the coordination between the various differentiated subunits necessary to get the job done.

Hard line versus dotted line

Consider who reports to whom on a formal basis (hard line) and who works for the project but formally reports outside the project organization (dotted line).

Staffing: Who do you need?

The triad at the top

It has been suggested by a corporate executive that every project involves three perspectives: a technical and business perspective, a political perspective, and a personal or people perspective. Each of these perspectives must be represented at the top of a project and each is critical.

These perspectives may be embodied in the project manager but even the most skilled project manager needs someone with whom he or she can discuss the technical and business aspects of the project, someone who has access to and understands the political power of the larger organization, and someone who can pull him or her up from the depths of depression almost always encountered in managing a project.

It is also important that the project be discussed, planned, and reviewed from these three broad perspectives. Therefore, this executive recommends that a triad of senior individuals be developed as a decision-making body within the project.

Technical confidant

Political confidant

Personal confidant

In addition to the triad at the top, the project manager needs:

Subordinate commanders

The troops

Picking your team

Who has the necessary information?

Who is available? Working with line managers?

Who is needed politically?

Bring on those who have good connections and reputations. Include those whose support will be critical to success and will be needed for implementation down the line.

Who is needed technically?

Who is needed personally?

How many people are needed?

What level of homogeneity is required?

Less homogeneity may result in more numerous and creative ideas, but also more conflict and increased time spent to make decisions. Consider trade-offs.

Using the network of alliances

How do you get your team members without resorting to a draft? The project manager does not have unilateral authority in the project effort; he or she frequently negotiates with the functional managers.

The flow of authority (and influence) is more a network of alliances among the project participants than a recurring delegation of power among the chain of superiors and subordinates in the various hierarchies. Keep in mind that this network of alliances depends heavily upon the reputation of the individual as reflected in his or her professional achievements.

8. Team-Building

It is critical that a project manager know what constitutes an effective team, as well as what leadership skills and activities are required to develop one. This chapter reviews the attributes of successful teams and team leaders, and traces team development through its four stages.

The attributes of effective teams

Commitment to a common course, standards, and goals

Agreement on expectations for the team

Commitment to common goals

Assumed responsibility for work to be done

Team values integrated with member values

Active and open exchange of information

Honest and open communication

Common access to information

Climate of trust

All members feel included

Differences of opinion are encouraged and freely expressed

Positive intergroup relations

Mistakes are treated as sources of learning

Mutual perception that everyone on the team is important to success

> *General feeling that one can influence what happens*
>
> *Mutual influence among all group members*
>
> *Interdependence of members*

Mutual concern for team members

Efficient use of each member's time (do not diminish group effectiveness by gathering them all for every situation)

Broad support for group decisions

Win-win approach to conflict resolution

Focus on group process/procedures as well as results

Effective work methods/procedures

Effective leadership

Benefits of teamwork

Improved communication

Better use of human resources

More creativity

Better leadership development

Improved job satisfaction

Attributes of successful team leaders

Recognize the whole is greater than the sum of the parts.

Realize that sharing power increases their own power.

Are not threatened by sharing power.

Place emphasis on the team-building process continually.

Developing effective teams

All group members on an effective team will exhibit certain skills and activities. These pertain to both project tasks and team maintenance.

Task or performance-related skills and activities

1. Initiating activity

   Proposing strategy, ideas, structure, or procedures

2. Giving information

   Relating experiences, expressing opinions, answering questions, providing facts

3. Requesting information

   Requesting data, opinions, and ideas

4. Adaptive problem solving

   Building upon the ideas of others, solving problems within established structure

5. Innovative problem solving

   Proposing novel ideas or ways of looking at issues. Playing "devil's advocate"

6. Generating and evaluating alternatives

Cost/benefit analysis of alternatives, working through issues

Team relationship or maintenance skills and activities

1. Involving others

Making sure every one participates

2. Gate-keeping

Summarizing progress, balancing the flow of participation, identifying issues

3. Listening

Hearing and attempting to understand others' points of view

4. Resolving differences

Offering alternatives when in conflict, collaborating, modifying positions, helping others work through disagreements

5. Climatizing

Being friendly and responsive, encouraging others, accepting others

6. Positive critique

Providing feedback, evaluating climate and progress

The four stages of team development

Team development/creation stages are guided through the use of specific leader actions and behaviors as situations change.

There are four identifiable stages of group or team development, and every team goes through these stages in order. The time required for each stage will vary from team to team.

Below are listed the characteristics of each stage, the typical concerns of team members during the first two stages, and some suggestions for appropriate actions of the project manager or leader during each stage.

Stage 1 – Forming

Characteristics

Group has generally positive expectations.

Group is moderately eager to get at task.

Task accomplishment is low due to high task and interpersonal anxiety.

Task anxiety is high.

Team member concerns

What is the group's purpose?

What are the group's goals?

What are the top priorities?

Who are the other members?

What are they like?

How will I fit in?

How much will I involve myself?

How much will I involve others?

Will my needs be included in group's goals?

Leader's actions

Decide on and communicate your vision of what the team should be. Define group purpose, goals, and priorities, involving all members for input, and having consensus on the purpose, goals, and priorities selected.

Communicate your philosophy of management.

Remain high task- and low relationship-oriented.

Be directive, as the group is dependent on authority.

Demand structure.

Get members involved.

Clarify the skills of the group and its members.

Stage 2 – Storming

Characteristics

Goals and structure are becoming clear.

Group skills are increasing gradually.

Task accomplishment is increasing slowly.

Motivation can drop due to:

discrepancy between members' hopes and reality

dissatisfaction with dependence on authority

members frustrated and angry

negative reactions to the leader.

Team member concerns

What is my role?

What are my responsibilities?

What procedures should we follow?

How much control will I try to take?

How much control will I allow others?

Leader's actions

Be task- and relationship-oriented.

Involve team in developing strategies to meet team objectives.

Define roles, responsibilities, and procedures.

Involve team in solving problems.

Continue to be highly directive.

Redefine tasks to be achieved.

Acknowledge and tolerate dissatisfaction, but do not become defensive and take it personally.

Be supportive.

Begin development of task skills to share leadership.

Stage 3 – Norming

Characteristics

Productivity continues to steadily rise.

Expectations have fallen in line with reality.

Dissatisfaction decreases dramatically.

Structure is clear.

Progress is clear.

Relationships are rebuilt and become settled.

Cohesion begins to develop.

Accepted behaviors are clarified.

The limits to individual roles are tested.

Leader's actions

Focus on being high relationship- and low task-oriented.

Involve team in key decisions where its input is most helpful and constructive.

Support the group in its development.

Acknowledge the progress of the group.

Stage 4 – Performing

Characteristics

The group is positive and eager.

Group productivity is high.

Group pride is higher.

Group confidence is high.

Members are able to work autonomously.

The leader's special status is eliminated.

Leader's actions

Maintain low task- and low relationship-orientation.

Communicate openly and freely.

Focus energy on results.

Recognize and support members' competence and accomplishment.

Support the autonomous functioning of the group.

Help group execute, follow through, and follow up.

Review progress in meeting tactical and strategic goals as a team periodically.

Executing, monitoring, and correcting

9. Running the Project

Executing

Maximize coordination among groups

1. Make sure that everyone understands the project plan.

2. Detail a clear chain of command for the project.

3. Maintain a high level of horizontal communication.

4. Use liaisons continually to ensure proper communication flow.

Use a visibility room

If possible, have a room in which current project status information is posted. This room should be open to everyone associated with the project. It should contain

1. Project plans

2. Current status of all open work packages

3. A list of issues, problems, and actions

Set up formal committees to handle specific functions and project areas at different levels

1. General management committee

   Project-related senior project or task managers, to improve horizontal communication and coordination across groups

2. Multiple level management committee

   Top managers and their immediate subordinates, to improve vertical communication and coordination

3. Special area committees

   Managers within the project with specific areas of interest

When working with committees, meet first with your subordinate managers, then with their subordinates.

Monitoring

Controlling work flow

Assign tasks

Use your responsibility matrix.

Set goals

Monitor progress

Break tasks into steps with deadlines, budget limits, and quality criteria, and monitor progress at intervals. Use the work breakdown structure and work packages.

Formal reviews and feedback

Management reviews

User/customer reviews

Project team reviews

External audits

Feedforward control

To achieve more effective control, it is necessary to reduce the magnitude of the error. To avoid the problems inherent in the response time of a feedback system, deviations should be anticipated. The only way to do this, short of using a crystal ball, is to monitor the critical inputs to a project and the ongoing project processes. If we watch changes in inputs and processes, we can determine if these would eventually cause failure to achieve desired goals. Time will then be available to take corrective actions.

There can be no doubt that feedforward is largely an attitude toward the analysis and solution of problems. It is the recognition that feedback information is just not adequate for management control and that a shift must be made away from emphasis on quickly available data on final results to quickly available data on those input and process variables that lead to final results. It is a means of seeing problems as they develop and not looking back—always too late—to see why a planning target was missed.

Personal observation

The project manager who relies wholly on budgets, charts, reports, ratios, auditors' recommendations, and other such necessary control devices, sits, so to speak, in a soundproof control room reading dials and manipulating levers. Such a manager can hardly expect to do a thorough job of control.

Keys to schedule control

Project and personnel commitments

Frequent milestones

"Razor-sharp" milestones

Good communication

Dealing with schedule problems

Ensure routine detection of problems.

Finding and fixing problems as early as possible is the only way to ensure project success. Problems are opportunities to improve the project. Make sure that problem finding is rewarded, not punished—don't shoot the messenger.

Hold project review meetings.

Encourage advance notice.

Advise owners and management of unavoidable delays as soon as possible.

Cost control

Use the "earned value concept" to monitor completion of work packages, as follows:

Compare the value (budgeted cost) of work packages completed against the value (budgeted cost) of work packages planned to be completed at this time, and calculate the schedule variance expressed in dollars.

Have we done more, the same, or fewer dollars worth of work up to this time than we had planned to do?

Compare the actual cost of completed work packages with the budgeted (planned) cost of the completed work packages to see the cost variance.

Has the cost of work actually completed been more, the same, or less than we had planned to spend for this work?

Correcting

Identification and correction of problems can be accomplished through a deviation analysis/potential problem analysis process.

Early identification of deviations/problems

After-the-fact damage control is very difficult. To keep ahead of problems:

Encourage early warning.

Communicate.

Manage by walking around.

Recovery analysis

Defining the problem

What exactly is the deviation or potential problem?

Where is it?

What is its extent?

When was it first noticed?

What specifically does it affect?

Has it occurred before? What was done then?

Finding the solution

What are the options?

Which option do the facts and experience favor?

Who can contribute to evaluating and effecting the best solution?

Can this option be effected without creating further problems?

What will the overall effect be on cost and schedule?

Is the option a cure or a palliative?

If the latter, what is the permanent solution?

Is a permanent solution required at that point?

Implementing the solution

Inform management and users/owners.

Ask for help if required. Problems do not improve with age.

Implement the "best" option.

Don't waste energy finding the "guilty" party. It contributes nothing to recovery from a problem. Therefore, it is dysfunctional to expend effort and resources to this end.

How to get in trouble

1. Not asking questions
2. Not believing what you hear
3. Refusing to take ownership of problems

4. Delaying in bringing problems to the attention of upper management

5. Receiving weak support by technical functional groups or working with technical groups that have weak capabilities

10. Reporting and Closedown

A project is remembered by its product, its documentation, and in the way in which the individuals and organizations involved were acknowledged for their work. In the final days of work, don't let the drive for production of the product obscure the need to formally complete all aspects of the project.

Reporting

One of the key responsibilities for the project manager is to ensure good reporting. Focus on:

- Right information
- Right people
- Right time
- Right format

What to report, to whom

Upward

Status

Problems, impact, and "get well plans"

Organizational issues

Warning flags

Future work

Downward

Program status

Project status

Cross-project problems/impacts

Future plans

Changes to the plan

Praise and honors

Horizontal

Cross-program information

Cross-organizational buy-in

Communication with customers

Reporting modes

Choose a reporting format that is appropriate for the material and for the organization and individuals you are addressing. How important is accuracy? Confidentiality? Will the information be transmitted to others?

Reporting options include:

Formal

Informal

Written

Electronic

Verbal

Closedown

Have a closedown plan as part of your overall project plan.

Keep it up to date.

Re-coordinate it as closedown approaches.

Give it good visibility.

The program closedown plan should cover issues including:

Delivering the product

Retention and/or archiving of data, plans, samples, etc.

Security closeout

Facility and space reallocation

Subcontractor closeout

Staff re-assignment

Staff performance evaluations

Final documentation

Follow-on work

11. International Projects

To some extent, international projects are a special case. All of the ideas, techniques, and suggestions in the first ten chapters apply to international projects. However, there are a number of additional factors that must be addressed when managing a project in a foreign country.

It is essential to recognize that in much of the world, American values, ethics, methods, and practices are not the norm. Especially in developing countries, normal business practices are often quite different from what is common in the US.

Culture

Different cultures are different. It is easy to fall into the trap of thinking that "we are all just people, so we can't be that different." But, the truth is that the differences can easily cause major problems for your project. People in different cultures think differently. Even if there is no language barrier, there are likely to be differences in ways of making decisions, in work style, in ways of expressing approval and disapproval, in expectations of the leader/manager, in bringing about change in the organization, etc. In many Asian countries, for example, social harmony is an important cultural value. As a result, disagreement and disapproval are seldom expressed directly.

This can lead to extreme misunderstandings. This author once made a presentation concerning a major change in a project plan. At the end of the presentation, the senior manager in charge of the project stated, "That was a wonderful presentation. I especially liked the new plan. But, before we sign the change agreement, could you show us another option that might be a bit lower in cost? Don't change the plan you presented, but just let me see another view." At the time, it seemed like we were very near an agreement. In fact, the senior manager's statements were a total rejection of the new plan and the project was delayed more than two months while we tried to reach agreement.

Language

Don't underestimate the impact of language differences. Even if the people you are working with are fluent in English and have been educated at US universities, there is still a high probability that misunderstandings will occur. This is especially true when abstract concepts are being discussed. This author once spent most of a full day with several Japanese colleagues trying to figure out what the Japanese equivalent of a "social group" was. The literal translation was easy, but the concept didn't seem to work.

Professional translators can help, but many times they are not familiar with technical ideas, concepts, and jargon. Thus, there is still room for misunderstandings. One technique we have used with a good deal of success in meetings with participants from two cultures is to use dual note takers. We do this with a pair of flip charts. One flip chart is used for notes in English, the other for notes in the other language. A bilingual translator keeps the notes in the language the current speaker is not using. Either the speaker or another member of his/her language group keeps the notes in that language. In that the flip charts are visible to all the participants, all those with dual language capability can suggest corrections and additions.

If at all possible, try to find someone who is bilingual and bicultural. By bicultural I mean someone who has lived for extended periods in both cultures. Such a person, especially if he or she has a technical background in the area of your project, can be an extremely valuable resource.

Work Ethic

Especially if project work is to be done by members of the client organization or local subcontractors, it is often critical to be aware of and understand the accepted local work standards for both quality and quantity of work. There are probably general standards within the overall culture as well as specific standards within the client organization. These standards often are considerably different from accepted practice in the US. Standards of work quantity and quality may also vary from time to time within a given organization depending on factors such as religion, political situation, weather, etc. In Muslim countries, for example, work hours often must be rearranged during the holy month of Ramadan and the major holiday period that follows.

Ignoring or not being aware of such differences can cause problems in several ways. The first and most obvious is the impact on schedule and budget estimates. The second is the potential for misunderstanding and conflict between project management and the workers. Setting up a project schedule based on five, eight-hour workdays per week when the workers expect to work and be paid for six, ten-hour workdays per week can cause a huge range of problems of both types.

Ethics, etc.

Normal or accepted standards of business practice vary greatly throughout the world. What may be considered normal business practice in one country may be illegal in another. A US company doing a project in a foreign country will probably be subject to both US law and the laws of the foreign country. The US Foreign Corrupt Practices Act outlines what are and are not allowed practice under US law. The rules under local law are often less clear. Legal representation by a local firm is often advisable to help clarify the situation.

Legal and Tax Issues

This may be obvious, but it is easy to forget that a project being conducted in a foreign country may be subject to various legal requirements such as registration as a business entity in that country as well as being liable for income, value-added, employment, and other taxes. Failure to comply with such requirements may be extremely costly.

Currency Exchange Rates

This is another obvious, but easy to forget, item. Often international projects will have a requirement that some, or all, of the project payments will be made in local currency. Fluctuations in exchange rates can wreak havoc with a project budget where some expenditures are required in different currencies. Employing experienced currency managers early in project planning and price negotiations can ward off some of the problems. In the late 1990s, many projects were devastated by the Asian economic difficulties.

Civil Unrest

Civil unrest can disrupt domestic projects as well as international projects. However, in most domestic projects, the project manager and the project team can readily access the resources of the home organization. When the project is located in a foreign country, the project team is much more isolated. The project manager is often the senior member from the home organization and, as such, must assume a range of responsibilities above and beyond those expected of a project manager in a domestic project situation:

- First, as a project manager you are clearly responsible for the physical safety of your project team. This may extend to the families of project team members.

- Second, you are responsible for protecting the interests of your home organization.

- Third, you are responsible for protecting the integrity of the project.

Information

In dealing with these responsibilities, it is critically important to have good information about the situation. Obtaining good information implies cultivating contacts with a range of sources. Certainly your own embassy is one place to obtain official information. US embassies in most developing countries maintain lists of US residents who they will notify if there is a general emergency. Thus, all members of the project team should register with the embassy. Most embassies maintain web sites that contain a wealth of information. It is also worthwhile to establish personal relationships with embassy staff members. Embassies will usually tend to overestimate the degree of danger, as they are responsible for protecting US citizens.

The local expatriate community is another source of information, although it is often made up of mostly rumors and speculation. However, it is often worthwhile to obtain the views of people from a range of organizations and countries.

The local government will probably tend to underestimate the degree of danger as they will not want to appear unable to provide security to foreigners. However, if you are able to establish personal relationships with government officials, you may be able to obtain insights not available elsewhere.

International organizations such as United Nations agencies, World Bank, and aid groups often are staffed with individuals with a great deal of international experience and knowledge. Thus, they are an extremely valuable source of information.

Your local counterparts can be a wonderful source of information. Building mutual trust and respect with your local counterparts is always critical in every project. It takes on extra importance in times of crisis.

The press will almost always exaggerate the magnitude of the crisis and the danger present. This is especially true for international television news. It is important to recognize that for friends and family as well as members of your home organization back in the US, CNN may be their only source of information. Thus, it is very important for you to provide as much information as possible to your home organization, family, and friends. In a crisis, there will be a great deal of concern for the safety of you and your project team. This can easily result in orders to stop the project or to evacuate the area because of perceived danger, when, in fact, little real danger is present.

Security Plan

In most projects, it is probably a good idea to have a safety and security plan. The importance of this obviously increases with the degree of danger present. This is true regardless of the source of the danger. It may come from the inherent nature of the work, from the remoteness of the project site, or from political instability. This plan should address current and potential safety and security risks and provide for action in the event of an emergency.

Appendix A – A Self Assessment of Team-Oriented Leadership

How do you rate yourself in each area? This questionnaire, adapted from Battelle's Assessment of Team-Oriented Leadership for Managers and Executives, includes 53 items covering nine key areas. These nine key areas were developed using a statistical technique called factor analysis from a much larger collection of items. More than 600 managers and executives from a range of organizations were rated by subordinates, supervisors, peers, clients, and themselves to establish a database. This database was analyzed to establish the fundamental dimensions or factors being measured. The dimensions include three factors associated with **Personal Characteristics** – *Integrity, Competence, and Drive;* two factors associated with **Focus and Knowledge** – *Your Own Organization and Your Customer's Organization;* two factors dealing with **People Leadership** – *Achieving Teamwork and Developing Individual Team Members;* and two factors dealing with **Task Leadership** – *Productivity and Decision Making.* These nine factors seem to cover the fundamentals of effective project management.

To help you think about your own effectiveness as a project manager, go through the items below and describe your own effectiveness. Try to be as candid and objective as possible. For each item, indicate your response by checking the box that best represents your view of your characteristics, competencies, and actions. If you are unsure of an answer, circle the letter "N."

1. Personal Characteristics

Rate the extent to which you exhibit these personal attributes and qualities:

1	2	3	N	*1 = not at all, 2 = to some extent, 3 = to a very large extent, N = not known*

Integrity

☐	☐	☐	N	Exhibiting high ethical standards of personal conduct
☐	☐	☐	N	Dealing honestly in every endeavor
☐	☐	☐	N	Following through with and keep commitments
☐	☐	☐	N	Keeping your word

Technical Competence

☐	☐	☐	N	Demonstrating proficiency in your field
☐	☐	☐	N	Knowing the technical requirements of the task
☐	☐	☐	N	Demonstrating competence on the job
☐	☐	☐	N	Applying technical knowledge and skills to achieve business results
☐	☐	☐	N	Using your knowledge and technical expertise to broaden the range of possible solutions

1	*2*	*3*	N	*1 = not at all, 2 = to some extent, 3 = to a very large extent, N = not known*

Drive

☐ ☐ ☐ N   Willingly exerting effort on behalf of your organization to achieve excellence

☐ ☐ ☐ N   Working hard at your job and enjoying it

☐ ☐ ☐ N   Taking initiative

☐ ☐ ☐ N   Showing determination in solving difficult problems

☐ ☐ ☐ N   Continuing to put forth effort in adverse circumstances

2. Focus and Knowledge

Rate your level of effectiveness in focusing on the needs and objectives of your customer's organization as well as the needs and objectives of your own organization:

1	*2*	*3*	N	*1 = ineffective, 2 = moderately effective, 3 = extremely effective, N = not known*

Customer Focus

☐ ☐ ☐ N   Demonstrating a clear commitment to customer service

☐ ☐ ☐ N   Working closely with customers and suppliers to define expectations and mutual responsibilities

☐ ☐ ☐ N   Understanding the customer's expectations

1	2	3	N	*1 = ineffective, 2 = moderately effective, 3 = extremely effective, N = not known*
□	□	□	N	Defining your organization's purpose in fulfilling customer expectations
□	□	□	N	Achieving/exceeding customer expectations

Focus on Your Organization

□	□	□	N	Understanding issues from the perspective of your overall organization
□	□	□	N	Contributing to the overarching goals of your company
□	□	□	N	Clearly defining problems/issues of cross-functional groups
□	□	□	N	Proactively assessing the impact of the ever-changing business environment

3. People Leadership

Rate your level of effectiveness in each of these skill areas:

1	2	3	N	*1 = ineffective, 2 = moderately effective, 3 = extremely effective, N = not known*

Achieving Teamwork

□	□	□	N	Promoting an environment of mutual trust and respect
□	□	□	N	Working with others as a team
□	□	□	N	Soliciting ideas from others before implementing an idea
□	□	□	N	Interacting comfortably and effectively with team members

1	2	3	N	*1 = ineffective, 2 = moderately effective, 3 = extremely effective, N = not known*
☐	☐	☐	N	Welcoming disagreement as a means to ensure complete information
☐	☐	☐	N	Listening effectively
☐	☐	☐	N	Recognizing unique contributions of others
☐	☐	☐	N	Avoiding "shooting the messenger"
☐	☐	☐	N	Resolving conflicts in a "win-win manner"
☐	☐	☐	N	Gaining the support of people who will implement your decisions

Developing Individual Team Members

1	2	3	N	
☐	☐	☐	N	Converting potential into performance
☐	☐	☐	N	Taking a personal interest in developing each team member
☐	☐	☐	N	Working with team members to develop individual career plans
☐	☐	☐	N	Encouraging and coaching others in self-development
☐	☐	☐	N	Providing advice and counsel on career development with each individual

4. Task Leadership

Rate your effectiveness in applying and sustaining these processes:

1	2	3	N	*1 = ineffective, 2 = moderately effective, 3 = extremely effective, N = not known*

Achieving Productivity

☐	☐	☐	N	Aligning team and organizational missions
☐	☐	☐	N	Assessing the situation and developing alternative courses of action
☐	☐	☐	N	Defining specific activities to be accomplished to fulfill the mission and objectives
☐	☐	☐	N	Developing specific plans to accomplish the goals of the team
☐	☐	☐	N	Integrating plans across functions
☐	☐	☐	N	Translating goals and objectives into specific tasks for assignment
☐	☐	☐	N	Working with the team to clarify expectations (e.g., results, standards, priorities)
☐	☐	☐	N	Focusing activity on achieving measurable outcomes

Decision Making

☐	☐	☐	N	Tackling the tough issues
☐	☐	☐	N	Assessing the situation and taking calculated risks
☐	☐	☐	N	Developing and implementing innovative strategies

1	2	3	N	*1 = ineffective, 2 = moderately effective, 3 = extremely effective, N = not known*
□	□	□	N	Understanding the parameters of risk-taking and when to elevate decisions to a higher level
□	□	□	N	Making decisions

Appendix B – The Project Manager's Checklist

Use the following checklist to track your progress, returning to the checklist during each stage of the project. It will help you pinpoint problem areas and maintain focus on key areas.

Getting started

☐ I understand the role of a project manager.

☐ I have assessed the project situation.

☐ I have identified the specific individuals whose support for the project is critical for its success.

☐ I have assessed my personal motivation and ability to be a project manager.

☐ I have selected and recruited my core team of two to four individuals to work with me on the up-front conceptualization.

☐ I have a clear, written charter from top management that details my responsibilities, authority, and degree of accountability.

Project mission and vision

☐ I understand the mission, values, and vision of my organization and of the customer/client organization.

☐ The project mission supports/is consistent with the above missions, values, and visions.

☐ The project team understands our organization's values and the customer/client organization's values.

☐ I understand and buy into the overall project mission.

☐ I have a clear vision of how this project will benefit the customer/client organization.

☐ I have articulated this vision in a clear, concise, written statement.

Project goals and objectives

☐ A set of specific goals and objectives has been developed that, if attained, will yield accomplishment of the project vision.

☐ Alternative approaches or strategies for accomplishing the goals and objectives have been generated and evaluated.

☐ A basic approach or strategy has been selected.

☐ Schedule milestones for attainment of goals and objectives have been developed.

Top management support

☐ I have discussed the project mission, vision, goals, objectives, and milestones with each of the top managers whose support is critical for project success.

☐ Each of the above top managers has publicly endorsed the project, its mission, vision, goals, objectives, and milestones.

☐ The project team has been granted the authority needed to successfully carry out the project.

Client/user consultation and ownership

☐ I have identified the key individuals in each of the client/user organizations.

☐ I have discussed the benefits of the project with each of these key individuals.

☐ I have discussed the limitations of the project with each of these key individuals.

☐ I have discussed the negative impacts of the project with each of these key individuals.

☐ I have solicited input from each of the client/user organizations.

☐ I understand the needs and concerns of each of the client/user organizations.

☐ Each of the client/user organizations has "signed up" to the requirements of the project.

☐ I am confident that the requirements will not change unrealistically during the project.

☐ The project and/or its products are part of the business plan of each client/user organization.

Planning

☐ A detailed work breakdown structure (WBS) has been developed for the project.

☐ A detailed responsibility matrix has been developed for the project.

☐ A detailed schedule with milestones and interdependencies has been developed for the project.

☐ A detailed, time-phased budget, linked to the WBS and schedule, has been established for the project.

☐ Key personnel needs (who, when) have been identified.

☐ A thorough risk analysis has been conducted.

☐ Contingency plans have been developed for all high-risk areas.

☐ Benefit/cost analyses for my organization and for each of the client/user organizations have been conducted.

☐ A user interface plan has been developed.

☐ Each of the above points has been incorporated into an overall project plan.

☐ The project plan has been reviewed and approved by all relevant individuals and organizations.

Communication

☐ A communication plan has been developed for the project.

☐ The communication plan includes all of the groups and individuals critical to project success.

☐ There is a published schedule of formal status briefings and reports.

☐ A system has been established for communicating changes, as they occur, to all of the project owners (management, project team, subcontractors, users, and customers).

☐ All owners and others associated with the project are aware of how they can make problems known to the project team.

Organizing

☐ A responsibility interface matrix has been developed, published, and communicated.

☐ Each individual and organization responsible for one or more work packages has received a statement of the work required.

☐ Interdependencies between and among work packages have been identified.

☐ Mechanisms are in place to ensure that the activities included in interdependent work packages will be integrated.

☐ Formal reporting relationships have been established throughout the project organization.

☐ Authority to make appropriate decisions has been delegated along with each work package.

☐ I am confident that each member of the project team understands both the extent and the limitations of his or her authority.

☐ I am confident that each member of the project team knows who they should contact for help if it is needed.

Staffing

☐ I have identified the knowledge, ability, style, and background requirements for all key positions on the project team.

☐ I have discussed the above requirements with the appropriate functional and line managers.

☐ Working with the functional and line managers, I have identified individuals to fill each of the project positions.

☐ I have spoken with each of the project team members about their roles, responsibilities, and authority with respect to the project.

☐ All project team members have "bought in" to the project vision, objectives, and plan.

☐ All project team members consider themselves to be owners of the project. (They speak about it as "our project.")

Executing

☐ All members of the project team (including senior management, customers, and subcontractors) understand:

　　☐ their individual and organizational roles in the project.

　　☐ the work/products/deliverables for which they are responsible.

　　☐ the interface/coordination requirements with other parts of the project.

　　☐ the quality, schedule, and budget requirements for their work.

□ A schedule of meetings has been established so that the status of the work-in-progress and planned work can be reported and discussed by the entire project team.

□ Project plans are sufficiently detailed that I can track overall project progress by comparing work packages completed against work packages planned to be completed and by comparing the actual costs of work packages completed against planned costs for these work packages.

□ I am confident that all team members will inform me of any problems they encounter early enough for me to take corrective action.

□ I am confident that the project will be completed within the planned quality, schedule, and budget parameters.

Appendix C – Messages from the Brass

In developing the *Survival Guide* we sought input not only from project managers but from the higher-ups who manage them. We asked these executives what messages they would like to pass along to current and prospective project managers.

Their remarks provide valuable insight into the upper management perspective, one that is often overlooked by managers in the midst of a project. We have organized these messages under headings that parallel the flow of a project—and of the *Survival Guide*.

What it takes to be a project manager

"Basic management skills are of critical importance."

"You have got to deliver. You can't just throw the product over the fence—it has got to work for the customer."

"Be decisive, but don't give orders. You must explain everything. The worst thing, though, is to fail to make a decision."

"Communicate upwards, downwards and sideways."

"Keep management informed."

"You've got to be able to sit back and think."

"Confront problems as they arise. Fear is self-generated and perceived, not a reflection of reality."

"Ask for help when you need it."

"Know your customer."

"Go to the job with fire! A project manager should be a good communicator with good management skills and an even temperament; a good leader, dedicated to continuous improvement; open-minded and looking to broaden his or her experience."

Getting started on the project

"Understand the project—what it is about and why it has the budget it does."

"Understand the scope of the project."

"Understand what it takes to execute the plan."

"Make sure you get the requirements from everyone involved."

"Recognize the constraints on the project."

"Acknowledge the necessity to improve processes."

"Assess the support base for the project, both inside and outside of your organization. Know the capacities and capabilities of vendors to support you."

"Build a database so that good estimates can be made. It's hard to feel like a winner when you miss estimates by orders of magnitude."

Charter and role of the project manager

"Get the resources needed to do the job."

"Understand the role from an upper management perspective. What are you being groomed for?"

"Understand the differences between the roles of the line manager and the project manager."

"Make sure that the user is committed and willing to stay involved throughout the project."

"Figure out a way to get at requirements and confirm them early on."

"Let project participants know that you are, in effect, running a business and have general management responsibilities. You are ultimately responsible."

"Make sure your team has the needed authority to do the job. If you don't have it, stop until you get it. Don't leave home without it!"

"If you don't have the necessary authority, take it. Most of the time it will be okay. This is required to succeed."

Ownership

"Involve everyone—senior management, customers, the project team, suppliers, subcontractors, support staff, and the ultimate users of the product."

"Remember that owners think and act differently from renters."

"Communication and training are key to getting user involvement."

"Don't underestimate the people issues when you are trying to change organizational culture."

"Have the customer actually manage the project."

Planning

"Planning, planning, planning, planning, planning, planning and planning."

"Develop the project plan. The project manager has to do this. It can't be done by the team."

"Project managers can get into trouble by failing to incorporate into the plan frequent reviews by the stakeholders. You need to get things in front of people, and the earlier, the better."

"A well thought-out plan leads to a detailed schedule. Remember that most senior managers are very schedule-conscious."

"Cost out everything in your plan, even for other organizations involved. Validate the budgets."

"A plan has to be flexible. Question the plan as you are following it, and change it when you need to."

Risk

"Make clear the risks the project entails. You may anger a lot of people, but they must understand the risks involved."

"Focus on the risks of failing to meet cost, schedule and project requirements."

"List all the known risks. Then develop abatement plans for each risk. What can you do right now to head off the risk? What will you do if the risk materializes? Allow reserves of both time and budget to deal with unknown risks."

"Communicate all known risks as widely as possible. Don't just hope for a miracle."

"Manage risk—don't let it manage you."

Organizing, staffing and team building

"Keep in mind the triad model for decision-making: You need a technical confidant, a political confidant, and a personal confidant. They are especially needed when you get in trouble."

"Pick the right people for specific jobs on the team."

"Select key people on both the business side and the technical side."

"Understand the technology, such as software, that supports the project. If you don't, get someone on your team who does."

"Select people and then train them."

"Schedule and plan specifically for team building."

"Know your team."

"Team performance requires a commitment from everyone involved."

"Create a team environment and work with consensus."

"Know how to manage people who don't work for you."

"Problems come from lack of team leadership."

Executing, monitoring and correcting

"Insist on quality. Quality is more important than schedule. Don't deliver something that won't do the job."

"Run the project in a disciplined manner. You can't skip details and you can't skip reviews."

"Maintain control of the project—the schedule, the budget, and the people."

"If you don't have regular monitoring and reviews, you will get in trouble. Projects are dynamic. You need to keep on top of changes and keep people involved."

"External audits can help a project rather than get in the way."

"Have a plan for resolution when conflicts arise."

"When a problem comes up, don't let organizational structure prevent you from talking to someone who can help you."

"Inform management about even small problems that you are addressing. Don't surprise them."

"Don't be alone. Share problems, and get help from above."

Index

A

accountability, 6
alliances and project teams, 42
ambiguity, 29, 30
approvals, 21
    See also ownership
assessing the project situation,
        3-5, 15–16
Augustine, Norman, 4
authority, 6, 11–12
    See also responsibilities

B

backward planning, 29, 30
budgets, 4, 56–57, 68

C

career choices, 3
charters, 6–8, 91
civil unrest, 69–71
closedown plan, 63
committees, 54
communication, 53, 54, 66–67,
        84–85

confidants, 41
constraints, 7–8
correcting problems, 56, 57–58,
        93–94
cost variance, 57
costs, 4, 56–57, 68
culture and international projects,
        65–66
currency exchanges, 68
customers, 5, 19, 24–26, 83

D

differentiation, 40
diversity, 40, 42
doomed projects, 3–5, 15–16

E

earned value concept, 56
embassies, 69
estimates, 15–16, 32
ethics, 67–68
exchange rates, 68

V

W